Order Code RL33776

CRS Report for Congress

Clean Air Issues in the 110th Congress: Climate Change, Air Quality Standards, and Oversight

Updated July 28, 2008

James E. McCarthy
Specialist in Environmental Policy
Resources, Science, and Industry Division

Congressional
Research
Service

Clean Air Issues in the 110th Congress: Climate Change, Air Quality Standards, and Oversight

Summary

Attention to environmental issues in the 110th Congress focused early and heavily on climate change — the state of the science, and whether (and, if so, how) to address greenhouse gas (GHG) emissions. Seventeen bills had been introduced to establish GHG emission caps as of June 2008, and hearings on climate change were held by at least 10 committees. The Lieberman-Warner bill to establish a cap-and-trade system for GHG emissions (S. 2191) was reported by the Senate Environment and Public Works Committee, May 20, 2008. Senate debate began on a modified version of the bill (S. 3036) June 2 but ended June 6, as the Senate failed to muster sufficient votes to invoke cloture.

Climate change hearings and markup have been among the highest priorities for the committees that have jurisdiction over air issues (principally Senate Environment and Public Works and House Energy and Commerce). Other clean air issues have been addressed largely through oversight of Administration actions. Oversight issues include how best to control emissions of mercury and other pollutants from electric power plants; whether EPA's new standards for ambient air concentrations of fine particulates and ozone and a proposed standard for lead adequately reflect the state of the science; and whether EPA's new process for setting ambient air quality standards politicizes what traditionally have been scientific judgments.

In addition to EPA, state governments and the courts have taken action on air issues that has stirred congressional interest. On April 2, 2007, the Supreme Court decided *Massachusetts v. EPA*, finding that EPA has authority under the Clean Air Act to regulate greenhouse gas emissions from new motor vehicles and requiring EPA to make a finding as to whether such emissions endanger public health or welfare. On February 8, 2008, the D.C. Circuit Court of Appeals, in *New Jersey v. EPA*, found EPA's approach to the regulation of power plant mercury emissions to be unlawful. On July 11, 2008, in *North Carolina v. EPA*, the D.C. Circuit vacated the Clean Air Interstate Rule (CAIR), which would have controlled emissions from power plants affecting air quality in downwind states. Other cases involving climate change, clean air standards, and the regulation of power plants are pending at the D.C. Circuit Court of Appeals and in a number of federal and state courts. Decisions in these cases may prompt hearings or legislation.

States interested in setting more stringent environmental standards are continuing to develop and implement regulations that go well beyond the requirements of federal law. Of particular interest is California's request for a waiver of federal preemption to control greenhouse gas emissions from cars and light trucks. On December 19, 2007, EPA announced that it would deny the waiver request, and the agency's Administrator signed a decision document formalizing his denial, February 29, 2008. California and more than a dozen other states are challenging the denial in court, and legislation has been introduced in both the Senate (S. 2555) and the House (H.R. 5560) to overturn the Administrator's decision.

Contents

List of Tables

Clean Air Issues in the 110th Congress: Climate Change, Air Quality Standards, and Oversight

Introduction

Attention to environmental issues in the 110th Congress focused early and heavily on climate change. The shift of control from Republicans to Democrats in the new Congress altered the political dynamic concerning this issue, although the shift was not sufficient to result in enacted legislation. Hearings have been held by at least 10 committees, and 17 bills to cap emissions of greenhouse gases (GHGs) have been introduced.[1] One of the bills, was reported, May 20, 2008, by the Environment and Public Works Committee, and Senate debate on a modified version (S. 3036) began June 2, 2008. A motion to invoke cloture failed June 6, on a vote of 48-36. On the House side, the Speaker has urged quick action on legislation, and established a Select Committee on Energy Independence and Global Warming to highlight the issue, but no bills have proceeded to markup.[2]

Ten of the 17 GHG cap-and-trade bills introduced as of this writing would amend the Clean Air Act, generally establishing a new Title VII to address the issue. (For additional information on climate change legislation, see CRS Report RL33846, *Greenhouse Gas Reduction: Cap-and-Trade Bills in the 110th Congress*, by Larry Parker and Brent D. Yacobucci.) Whether or not climate change legislation would amend the Clean Air Act, climate change hearings and markup have been among the highest priorities for the committees that have jurisdiction over air issues (principally the Senate Environment and Public Works and House Energy and Commerce Committees). Other clean air issues have not been the main focus of attention, but they are being addressed, primarily through oversight of Administration actions.

This report provides a brief overview of the climate change issue as well as other Clean Air Act issues of interest in the 110th Congress.

---

[1] Twelve of the 17 would establish economy-wide cap-and-trade programs. The other five bills establish cap-and-trade programs for the electric utility sector only.

[2] CRS has more than 50 active reports on climate change issues. The reader is referred to the CRS home page for additional information.

Climate Change

Climate change (often referred to as global warming) has been of interest to the Congress on some level for more than 30 years. Hearings on the topic occurred as early as 1975, with as many as 250 additional hearings since that time. In 1992, the United States ratified the U.N. Framework Convention on Climate Change (UNFCCC), which established a goal of reducing developed countries' greenhouse gas emissions to 1990 levels by the year 2000. In 1997, the parties to the UNFCCC, as a first step to advance stronger measures, negotiated binding emission reductions for developed countries in the Kyoto Protocol. The United States subsequently rejected the Protocol, focusing instead on research and on voluntary emission reduction programs.[3] Despite these programs, U.S. emissions of greenhouse gases have continued to climb: in 2005, U.S. emissions were 16% higher than in 1990.[4]

In recent years, Congress has expressed renewed interest in climate issues for several reasons. Perhaps the most important factor has been the continued strengthening of the science supporting the connection between emissions of greenhouse gases and climate changes, including mounting evidence that glaciers and polar ice caps are shrinking, global average temperatures are rising, and other climate-related phenomena are occurring. (For a summary of the science, see CRS Report RL33849, *Climate Change: Science and Policy Implications*, by Jane A. Leggett.) In response, about two dozen states have entered into regional agreements to address the issue. (For a summary of state actions, see CRS Report RL33812, *Climate Change: Action by States to Address Greenhouse Gas Emissions*, by Jonathan L. Ramseur.) There has also been a shift in attitude on the part of some in industry, prompted in part by the growing patchwork of state-level and foreign requirements. New business coalitions have formed to urge Congress to address the problem, or to influence any legislation that Congress might consider.[5]

---

[3] The Bush Administration has focused voluntary efforts on reducing the "greenhouse gas intensity" of the economy, i.e., the amount of greenhouse gases emitted per unit of economic activity. GHG intensity has consistently declined since the 1970s; but the rate of economic growth has outpaced the intensity reductions, leading to a steady increase in emissions.

[4] World emissions also grew in the period, although comprehensive data for world greenhouse gas emissions are not available for the same time period. According to the World Resources Institute, world emissions of CO_2 (not including other greenhouse gases) grew 21% from 1990 to 2003.

[5] For example, see "Businesses Call on Congress to Act in 2007," *Daily Environment Report*, January 23, 2007, p. A-1. The article reported that a coalition of 10 large U.S. energy and manufacturing firms joined environmental organizations in calling on Congress to approve legislation in 2007 that would create an economywide cap-and-trade system to cut the nation's greenhouse gas emissions, saying they would support legislation that would cap U.S. emissions at 2007 levels by 2012 and gradually reduce them by 60 percent to 80 percent by 2050. The companies included Alcoa, BP America, Caterpillar Inc., Duke Energy, DuPont, General Electric, Florida Power & Light, the Lehman Brothers global investment bank, PG&E, and PNM Resources. Since the coalition's formation, other large companies, including all three domestic auto manufacturers and ConocoPhillips, the nation's second largest oil company, have joined the coalition. For more information, see

(continued...)

Congress was already beginning to respond to these changes before the 2006 elections. In the 109th Congress, the Senate passed a Sense of the Senate resolution that acknowledged a "growing scientific consensus" that human activity is a substantial cause of greenhouse gas accumulation in the atmosphere, causing average temperatures to rise, and called for a mandatory, market-based program to limit greenhouse gas emissions.[6] On a complicated issue such as greenhouse gas limits, the devil is in the details: agreement on general principles does not necessarily presage agreement on detailed legislative proposals. One detailed proposal reached the Senate floor before this Congress: the McCain-Lieberman bill (S. 1151 in the 109th Congress, S. 139 in the 108th) would have established a mandatory, market-based greenhouse gas reduction program. It was debated in the 109th Congress as an amendment to the Energy Policy Act of 2005 (S.Amdt. 826) and defeated by a 38-60 vote; as stand-alone legislation, it was defeated 43-55 in the 108th Congress.[7]

In the 110th Congress, there has been new impetus. In the Senate, the Chairs of both the Environment and Public Works Committee and the Energy and Natural Resources Committee announced their intentions to move legislation; the Environment and Public Works Committee approved S. 2191, amended, December 5, 2007, by a vote of 11-8. The bill was reported (S.Rept. 110-337) May 20, 2008, and Senate debate on a modified version of the bill (S. 3036) began June 2. A motion to invoke cloture failed, however, June 6, on a vote of 48-36. In the House, the Speaker has urged quick action, but markup of legislation has not occurred. The Energy and Commerce Committee, which has jurisdiction, has held a number of hearings and has posted four white papers describing a possible cap-and-trade program, but the same committee has jurisdiction over the related issue of energy policy and focused its efforts in the first session on the passage of landmark energy legislation (P.L. 110-140), which was signed by the President December 19, 2007. There has been further attention to climate change bills in the second session of the Congress, but a significant number of questions, both procedural and substantive, remain.

Legislative Issues

Should Greenhouse Gases Be Regulated as Air Pollutants? The relationship of climate change legislation to the more traditional air pollution programs of the Environmental Protection Agency (EPA) is one such question. In brief, should greenhouse gases (particularly carbon dioxide) be considered air

---

[5] (...continued)
[http://www.us-cap.org/]. See also, "Exxon Mobil Greens Up Its Act," *Fortune*, January 26, 2007, which notes: "In its ubiquitous corporate advertising, the company is talking about what actions should be taken to reduce greenhouse gas emissions, instead of questioning the science of climate change.... That's a turnabout from the late 1990s and early 2000s when Exxon led the opposition to the Kyoto Protocols and provided funding for think tanks that challenged mainstream science."

[6] The resolution, which was Section 1612 of the Senate energy bill (H.R. 6, as amended by S.Amdt. 866), was not included in the enacted version of the bill, P.L. 109-58.

[7] The bill that was defeated was S. 139, as amended by S.Amdt. 2028.

pollutants subject to regulation under the Clean Air Act, or are they more properly considered a side-effect of the use of fossil fuels to produce energy?

The answer to this question affects jurisdiction over a climate change program (particularly in the Senate, where both the Energy and Natural Resources Committee and the Environment and Public Works Committee have considered greenhouse gas legislation). It could determine whether EPA, the Department of Energy, or some other agency would administer an enacted climate change program. And it might affect whether states have authority independent of the federal government to control certain greenhouse gas emissions.

Over the years, EPA has taken both sides of this issue. Under the Clinton Administration, the agency's General Counsel argued that CO_2 is an air pollutant, and thus could be regulated under the existing authority of the Clean Air Act. The agency did not actually propose such regulation; it simply maintained that it would have the authority to do so if it chose. Under the Bush Administration, a new General Counsel argued the opposite, maintaining that Congress had clearly distinguished CO_2 from other air pollutants and, while authorizing research and data collection under the existing Clean Air Act, had expressly decided not to regulate the pollutant. (For a further discussion of these issues, see CRS Report RL32764, *Climate Change Litigation: A Growing Phenomenon*, by Robert Meltz.) The Bush Administration has also intervened in court to argue that controlling CO_2 and other greenhouse gas emissions from automobiles is equivalent to setting fuel economy standards (a regulatory authority that Congress reserved for the federal government), not controlling air pollution (where states have a regulatory role).

In its April 2, 2007 decision in *Massachusetts v. EPA*,[8] the Supreme Court resolved the legal aspects of this issue, finding:

> The Clean Air Act's sweeping definition of "air pollutant" includes "*any* air pollution agent or combination of such agents, including *any* physical, chemical ... substance or matter which is emitted into or otherwise enters the ambient air...." ... Carbon dioxide, methane, nitrous oxide, and hydrofluorocarbons are without a doubt "physical [and] chemical ... substances[s] which [are] emitted into ... the ambient air." The statute is unambiguous.[9]

Thus, the Court found no doubt that the Clean Air Act gives EPA the authority to regulate greenhouse gases (in this case, from new motor vehicles), although the specifics of such regulation might be subject to agency discretion. (For further discussion of the Court's decision, see CRS Report RS22665, *The Supreme Court's Climate Change Decision: Massachusetts v. EPA*, by Robert Meltz.)

As noted, 10 of the 17 bills introduced as of this writing to cap greenhouse gas emissions would amend the Clean Air Act. In order to sidestep the complexities of treating GHGs as traditional pollutants, they generally establish a new Title VII to establish a separate program for greenhouse gas emissions. In this respect, the bills

---

[8] [http://www.supremecourtus.gov/opinions/06pdf/05-1120.pdf]

[9] Ibid., Opinion of the Court, p. 26.

emulate the 1990 Clean Air Act Amendments, which established separate titles to deal with acid precipitation (Title IV) and stratospheric ozone depletion (Title VI).

Should Legislation Focus on Individual Sectors, the Economy as a Whole, or Both? Most of the bills dubbed "climate change" bills would establish economy-wide programs to reduce greenhouse gas emissions. But recent Congresses, including the current one, have also seen dozens of bills aimed at the emissions of individual sectors, notably electric utilities, cars and trucks, electrical appliances, and commercial or government buildings. Together, these sectors account for the lion's share of energy use and GHG emissions. Electric utilities account for about 40% of U.S. emissions of CO_2. Transportation (of which the dominant portion is cars and trucks) accounts for about one-third. Appliances, other electrical equipment, and buildings all play important roles as consumers of energy; thus, reducing their energy use through efficiency standards, better insulation, etc., can be important means of reducing GHG emissions.

If the focus is on individual sectors rather than the economy as a whole, the likelihood is that new legislation to reduce GHGs would not amend the Clean Air Act, and the resulting regulatory programs would be implemented and administered by agencies other than EPA. For example, the Corporate Average Fuel Economy (CAFE) standards, which have regulated the fuel economy of automobiles and light trucks since the mid-1970s, are set and administered by the National Highway Traffic Safety Administration of the Department of Transportation. P.L. 110-140, signed by the President December 19, 2007, strengthened these standards for the first time since 1975. The new standards require that new vehicles achieve about a 40% improvement in fuel economy by 2020. The law also requires the Secretary of Transportation to establish standards for each model year, beginning with MY 2011. Appliance efficiency standards are set by the Department of Energy (DOE). These standards were also strengthened in P.L. 110-140. Other potential elements of a GHG reduction program, such as building codes, are administered by state and local governments, although DOE provides input to commercial building codes under provisions of the Energy Policy Act of 1992.[10] Power plants represent a particularly complicated sector, which, depending on the source of power, may be regulated by the Nuclear Regulatory Commission, the Federal Energy Regulatory Commission, or EPA, with a major role also for state governments. (For a discussion of federal programs and policies, see CRS Report RL31931, *Climate Change: Federal Laws and Policies Related to Greenhouse Gas Reductions*, by Brent D. Yacobucci and Larry Parker.)

Is Cap-and-Trade the Best Approach? The complexity and sheer number of measures that might need to be taken in order to have a significant impact on GHG emissions in sector-specific approaches leads many to suggest an economy-wide approach, in which a decreasing annual emissions cap is established, and emission allowances are distributed or sold to major emitters. As the cap (and hence, the number of allowances) is gradually ratcheted down, markets would determine who

---

[10] See CRS Report RL31931, *Climate Change: Federal Laws and Policies Related to Greenhouse Gas Reductions*, by Brent D. Yacobucci and Larry Parker, p. 10. P.L. 110-140 also strengthened DOE's authority regarding building energy efficiency standards.

reduces emissions: companies that could do so at low cost would have incentives to take action; companies with fewer or more costly options could buy allowances to cover excess emissions. (For a more complete discussion of these issues see CRS Report RL33799, *Climate Change: Design Approaches for a Greenhouse Gas Reduction Program*, by Larry Parker.)

Such cap-and-trade programs have an enviable reputation, largely based on the success of the Clean Air Act's acid rain program. That program imposed a cap on sulfur dioxide emissions for a limited number of electric power plants in 1995, and in 2000 lowered the cap and expanded coverage to more plants. It met its emission reduction goals at low cost, with virtually 100% compliance, and with minimal administrative oversight. The success of the program was at least partly the result of the favorable circumstances in which it was implemented: the reduction targets were easily met because of an abundant supply of cheap low-sulfur coal; there were only about 1,000 entities (power plants) covered by the trading program, making it simple and inexpensive to monitor and administer; and most of the regulated entities were allowed 10 years to achieve compliance, by which time, early reductions had generated an enormous number of extra allowances that helped lubricate the trading system.

Some other trading programs have not been as successful. Southern California's Regional Clean Air Incentives Market (RECLAIM), for example, which was implemented in 1994 to reduce emissions of nitrogen oxides (NOx) and sulfur dioxide (SO_2) in the Los Angeles area, saw a 50-fold increase in NOx allowance prices during the 2000-2001 California energy crisis. To permit its continued functioning and allow utilities to use backup power generators, electric utilities were removed from the RECLAIM system, charged a flat fee of $15,000 per ton for excess emissions, and subjected to new command and control requirements (i.e., the type of regulation the trading system was designed to avoid). The European GHG trading system (EU-ETS), established to help European Union countries meet their Kyoto Protocol targets, has also seen wild swings in short-term allowance prices during its start-up years, making planning and decision-making difficult for participating entities.[11]

A U.S. cap-and-trade system for GHG emissions would face a number of challenges. First, with the exception of electric utilities, sources of GHGs have not been generally required to monitor or report their GHG emissions; what we know about sources is based, for the most part, on estimates. Thus, a monitoring requirement would need to be established to serve as a basis for any future reduction scheme, whether cap-and-trade or not. Second, decisions would need to be made regarding the comprehensiveness of any program: what economic sectors to include, what to establish as a small emitter exemption, etc. Again, this problem is not unique to cap-and-trade, but it assumes increasing importance if one is designing any economy-wide approach. Third, there is a wide array of issues related to the distribution or sale of allowances, including what year to choose as the base year against which to measure emission reductions; what criteria or method to use to

---

[11] For additional information on the EU trading system, see CRS Report RL33581, *Climate Change: The European Union's Emissions Trading System (EU-ETS)*, by Larry Parker.

allocate allowances; whether to auction allowances to existing sources of emissions or give them away; whether to establish reserves for new sources; etc. Fourth, in order to prevent wild swings in allowance prices, a variety of flexibility mechanisms have been suggested, including a "safety valve" (a price at which the regulatory authority would sell additional allowances if the market cost rose above predicted levels); the banking of excess allowances (achieved through early reductions) for later use; borrowing authority; etc. Others have proposed a floor below which prices would not be allowed to fall, to reduce risk for sources that make GHG reductions. If a safety valve or floor were established, the price of additional allowances and/or the floor price would be key determinants of the stringency of the program. Fifth, there are a number of issues related to whether and how to permit international trading of allowances. Many of the least cost GHG reduction options may be in developing countries, but verification of the baseline emissions and of the continued application of emission controls could pose challenges to the regulatory authority in such cases. Similar questions are raised by potential domestic or international offsets to emissions, in the form of sequestration activities.[12]

What Role for Carbon Taxes? The complications of establishing a viable cap-and-trade program suggest to some (especially to those trained in economics) that the simplest approach to controlling emissions would be to impose a carbon or GHG tax. From the point of view of economic efficiency, administrative ease, and comprehensiveness, a carbon tax has many advantages, but Congress has found it difficult to impose new taxes, limiting support for this option. It is worth noting that the "safety valve" discussed in the cap-and-trade section above would function to some extent like a carbon tax, and might represent a compromise between these two options.

The Role of State Programs. Finally, as noted earlier, a number of states have begun programs to reduce GHG emissions. Although the federal government is challenging some of these, particularly those affecting mobile sources, states do have clear authority to regulate emissions from power plants, landfills, residential and commercial buildings, and other sources of GHGs. The extent to which such state programs might serve as national models is one issue; another is the degree to which a federal program might preempt state measures affecting similar sources.

California's Waiver Request

The question of federal preemption has already arisen under current law. California has adopted regulations requiring new motor vehicles to reduce GHG emissions, beginning in model year 2009. The standards require gradual reductions of GHG emissions until they are about 30% below the emissions of the 2002 fleet in

---

[12] For a broader discussion of issues faced in designing a GHG reduction program, see CRS Report RL33799, *Climate Change: Design Approaches for a Greenhouse Gas Reduction Program*, by Larry Parker. For information on how introduced bills address these and other issues, see CRS Report RL33846, *Greenhouse Gas Reduction: Cap-and-Trade Bills in the 110th Congress*, by Larry Parker and Brent D. Yacobucci.

2016.[13] Compliance would be determined by fleet averages, rather than by the emissions of individual vehicles, and the regulations provide additional flexibility, including averaging, banking, and trading of credits within and among manufacturers.

Although California finalized its regulations in 2005, the standards have not gone into effect because the state first needed to obtain a waiver of federal preemption from U.S. EPA. The Clean Air Act generally preempts states from adopting their own emission standards for mobile sources of air pollution, but it makes a conditional exception for California — whose air pollution problems have been more severe than those of other states, and whose emission control program pre-dated federal requirements. To obtain this exception, the state must be granted a waiver by the EPA Administrator. The act also permits other states to adopt standards identical to California's, if California is granted a waiver: 14 states have adopted identical standards.[14] Together, the states that have adopted the California standards represent nearly half the U.S. auto market, so there is broad interest in EPA's decision and a great deal at stake.

To obtain a waiver, California must meet four conditions laid out in CAA Section 209(b): the state must determine that its standards will be at least as protective of public health and welfare as applicable federal standards; and the EPA Administrator must weigh whether the state's determination in this regard is arbitrary and capricious; whether the state needs such standards to meet compelling and extraordinary conditions; and whether the standards and accompanying enforcement procedures are consistent with Section 202(a) of the Clean Air Act.

California appears to have a sound argument that it meets these tests. No federal standards address greenhouse gas emissions from mobile sources, so the requirement that the state's standards be at least as protective as federal standards would appear to be met. The state identified several compelling and extraordinary conditions that the standards are designed to address, and the state provided information describing technologies available to meet the standards, many of which are already available on vehicles, and addressed consistency with Section 202(a).

The legislative history of the waiver provision would also seem to support California's case. In the most recent amendment of Section 209(b), the House committee report stated: "The Administrator is not to overturn California's judgment

---

[13] A table showing the mandated reductions year-by-year can be found in the California Air Resources Board's *Regulations to Control Greenhouse Gas Emissions from Motor Vehicles, Final Statement of Reasons*, August 4, 2005, p. 8 at [http://www.arb.ca.gov/regact/grnhsgas/fsor.pdf].

[14] The 14 states are Arizona, Connecticut, Florida, Maine, Maryland, Massachusetts, New Jersey, New Mexico, New York, Oregon, Pennsylvania, Rhode Island, Vermont, and Washington. Under Section 177 of the act, states that have nonattainment or "maintenance" areas can adopt California's emission standards for mobile sources in lieu of federal standards. Every state except Hawaii, North Dakota, and South Dakota would be eligible to adopt California's standards under this so-called "piggyback' provision. Thus, there is broad interest in the California waiver decision and more at stake than would be the case if only California had adopted the regulations.

lightly. Nor is he to substitute his judgment for that of the State."[15] (For a further discussion, see CRS Report RL34099, *California's Waiver Request to Control Greenhouse Gases Under the Clean Air Act*, by James E. McCarthy and Robert Meltz.)

Nevertheless, the EPA Administrator announced on December 19, 2007, that he would deny the waiver request. According to press reports, the decision to deny the waiver was taken against the unanimous advice of the agency's technical and legal staffs.[16] In a letter to California's Governor Schwarzenegger on that date, the Administrator cited the signing earlier the same day of the Energy Independence and Security Act (P.L. 110-140), which established new fuel efficiency standards for motor vehicles, as providing a national approach to greenhouse gas emissions, a problem that, ne noted, is "fundamentally global in nature." He also contrasted the problems caused by GHGs to the local and regional air quality problems addressed by previous California waiver requests, more than 50 of which have been granted by EPA since the late 1960s.[17]

On February 29, 2008, the Administrator signed a formal decision document denying the waiver. (The decision document appeared in the March 6 *Federal Register*). In it, he based his denial on a finding that Section 209(b) was intended to allow California "to address problems that are local or regional," not global climate change. He also held that the effects of climate change in California are not compelling and extraordinary, as the statute requires, compared to the effects in the rest of the country.[18] On January 2, 2008, California and 15 other states filed suit challenging the Administrator's decision.

The auto industry, in addition to the Bush Administration, is opposed to the granting of a waiver. The industry maintains that there is effectively no difference between California and federal emission standards in their impact on criteria air pollutants, that the benefits of the GHG regulations are "zero", and that emissions

---

[15] U.S. House of Representatives, Committee on Interstate and Foreign Commerce, Clean Air Act Amendments of 1977, H.Rept. 95-294, May 12, 1977, pp. 301-302.

[16] "EPA Chief Denies Calif. Limit on Auto Emissions," Washington Post, December 20, 2007, p. A1. Documents shown to, and transcribed by, congressional staff have included numerous statements by senior EPA staff recommending that the Administrator grant the waiver; and the Administrator has not identified any staff recommendation suggesting denial. See U.S. Senate, Committee on Environment and Public Works, Hearings, January 24, 2008 and February 27, 2008.

[17] Letter of EPA Administrator Stephen L. Johnson to Governor Arnold Schwarzenegger, December 19, 2007, p. 1.

[18] U.S. EPA, "California State Motor Vehicle Pollution Control Standards; Notice of Decision Denying a Waiver of Clean Air Act Preemption for California's 2009 and Subsequent Model Year Greenhouse Gas Emission Standards for New Motor Vehicles," 73 *Federal Register* 12156, March 6, 2008.

will actually increase as a result of the regulations as consumers keep older, higher-emitting cars longer.[19]

If California were granted a waiver, there might be other impediments to the implementation of its standards, as industry opponents challenge EPA's authority in court. Already, in several court cases,[20] the issue has been raised whether EPA and California are prohibited from regulating greenhouse gases by the Corporate Average Fuel Economy (CAFE) requirements of the Energy Policy and Conservation Act of 1975 (EPCA). Under EPCA, the authority to set fuel economy standards is reserved for the federal government, and specifically, the National Highway Traffic Safety Administration. The auto industry maintains that the regulation of greenhouse gases is simply another method of regulating fuel economy, and, therefore, that California's GHG standards are preempted by EPCA. In the first of the cases to be tried, *Green Mountain Chrysler Plymouth Dodge Jeep v. Crombie*,[21] and *Association of International Automobile Manufacturers v. Crombie*,[22] now consolidated, the federal district court in Vermont ruled September 12, 2007, that the Clean Air Act/EPCA relationship is one of overlap, not conflict, and concluded that California and other states are not preempted by EPCA from setting mobile source GHG standards. In a second decision, *Central Valley Chrysler Jeep, Inc. v. Goldstone*,[23] a district court in the Ninth Circuit similarly rejected claims that California's regulation of GHG emissions from cars and trucks was precluded or preempted by EPCA. The first of these decisions has been appealed, and the other likely will be.

Following the Administrator's decision, legislation was introduced in both the Senate (S. 2555) and the House (H.R. 5560) to overturn the Administrator's denial. The Senate bill was reported, June 27 (S.Rept. 110-407). The bills would consider California's application for a waiver to be approved, notwithstanding any other provision of law.

Mass. v. EPA Endangerment Finding

As a result of the Supreme Court's decision in *Massachusetts v. EPA*, EPA was ordered to decide whether to regulate mobile source GHGs *nationally* under Section 202 of the CAA. The issue here is whether GHGs are pollutants that, in the words of Section 202, "cause, or contribute to, air pollution which may reasonably be anticipated to endanger public health or welfare." The Court's decision left EPA three options: (a) make a finding that motor vehicle GHG emissions may endanger public health or welfare, and issue emissions standards; (b) make a finding that such emissions do not endanger public health or welfare; or (c) decide that climate change

---

[19] Alliance of Automobile Manufacturers, "California Waiver Request," presentation materials from U.S. EPA public hearing, Sacramento, CA, May 30, 2007.

[20] The most important of these cases, because it challenges California's standards, as opposed to those adopted by one of the piggyback states, is Central Valley Chrysler Jeep, Inc. v. Goldstone, 456 F. Supp. 2d 1160 (E.D. Cal. 2006).

[21] No. 2:05-CV-302 (D. Vt. filed November 18, 2005).

[22] No. 2:05-CV-304 (D. Vt. filed November 18, 2005).

[23] No. 04-6663, 2007 Westlaw 4372878 (E.D. Cal. December 11, 2007).

science is so uncertain as to preclude making a finding either way (or cite some other "reasonable explanation" why EPA will not exercise its discretion either way).[24]

EPA has not spoken definitively on whether climate change endangers public health, but the agency appears to have already concluded that GHGs do affect welfare. Under the Clean Air Act, welfare is defined to include effects on soils, water, crops, vegetation, wildlife, weather, and climate. In his decision document on the California waiver request, which appeared in the *Federal Register*, March 6, 2008, the Administrator stated: "It is widely recognized that greenhouse gases have a climatic warming effect by trapping heat in the atmosphere that would otherwise escape to space."[25] He went on to enumerate impacts on temperature, precipitation, sea level rise, water resources, coastal communities, habitats, invasive species, air quality, and other factors.[26] Given these statements, it is hard to see how the agency can do other than issue an affirmative endangerment finding for welfare.

After the Supreme Court's decision last year, the Administrator (and the President, as well) gave every indication that they were on the way to making such a finding. The President, on May 14, 2007, said:

> Last month, the Supreme Court ruled that the EPA must take action under the Clean Air Act regarding greenhouse gas emissions from motor vehicles. So today, I'm directing the EPA and the Department of Transportation, Energy, and Agriculture to take the first steps toward regulations that would cut gasoline consumption and greenhouse gas emissions from motor vehicles...."[27]

In a briefing after the President's statement and at several Congressional hearings, the Administrator stated his intention to propose regulating GHGs from automobiles before the end of 2007.[28] EPA's Semiannual Regulatory Agenda, issued

---

[24] Justice Scalia's dissent characterizes EPA's three options similarly: 127 S. Ct. at 1472.

[25] 73 FR 12165.

[26] Ibid., pp. 12165-12168. It should be noted, however, that despite the clear statements about the effect of GHGs on welfare in the waiver document, a footnote at the outset of the discussion states: "This document does not reflect, and nothing in this document should be construed as reflecting, my judgment regarding whether emissions of GHGs from new motor vehicles or engines cause or contribute to air pollution 'which may reasonably be anticipated to endanger public health or welfare,' which is a separate question involving different statutory provisions and criteria; nor should it be construed as reflecting my judgment regarding any issue relevant to the determination of this question." (73 FR 12156, note 1)

[27] See "President Bush Discusses CAFE and Alternative Fuel Standards," White House Press Release, May 14, 2007, and "Executive Order: Cooperation Among Agencies in Protecting the Environment with Respect to Greenhouse Gas Emissions From Motor Vehicles, Nonroad Vehicles, and Nonroad Engines,"at [http://www.whitehouse.gov/news/releases/2007/05/20070514-4.html].

[28] See, for example, the Administrator's statement to the House Committee on Oversight and Government Reform, November 8, 2007, p. 58, at [http://oversight.house.gov/documents/20071115145634.pdf].

in December 2007, said the agency would "issue a notice of proposed rulemaking by the end of 2007 and a final rule by the end of October 2008."[29]

According to EPA staff, an endangerment of welfare finding was prepared and a proposed GHG emission standard was approved by the Administrator. The endangerment finding was sent to the White House Office of Management and Budget (OMB) somewhere between December 5 and December 8, 2007, and a proposed GHG emission standard was sent to the Department of Transportation.[30]

The endangerment finding and the proposed standards have not been issued, however, and the Administrator has recently begun the process all over with a request for information from the public (termed an "Advance Notice of Proposed Rulemaking," or ANPR). The ANPR was released July 11, 2008.[31] EPA staff have apparently been told that work was discontinued so that the agency's activities could be reassessed given enactment of the Energy Independence and Security Act (EISA, P.L. 110-140), which set new Corporate Average Fuel Economy (CAFE) standards for motor vehicles, which will reduce their GHG emissions. In the months after the bill's enactment, however, EPA staff were not asked to analyze whether passage of the law changed the analysis of the costs and benefits of the proposed GHG regulations.[32] Furthermore, as numerous commentators have noted, the passage of the new CAFE requirements does not affect EPA's obligation to issue a finding as to whether or not GHG emissions from mobile sources contribute to air pollution that endangers public health or welfare. In fact, Section 3 of EISA specifically states that nothing in the act supersedes the provisions of existing environmental law.

If the agency does eventually make an endangerment finding, it would still have substantial discretion in promulgating the actual standards to control GHGs. CAA section 202 does not explicitly impose any stringency or other criteria on GHG emission standards under the section. It says only that the Administrator "shall by regulation prescribe (and from time to time revise) ... standards applicable to the emission of any air pollutant...." Reflecting the apparently wide latitude EPA has in setting section 202 standards, commentators have suggested that EPA, following an endangerment finding, could set voluntary standards, or standards pegged to the CAFE standards for fuel economy. Presumably such standards would be subject to further review by the courts.

Congressional committees, especially the House Oversight and Government Reform Committee and the Senate Environment and Public Works Committee, have

---

[29] U.S. EPA, *Regulatory Plan and Semiannual Regulatory Agenda*, Sequence Number 136, "Rulemaking to Address Greenhouse Gas Emissions from Motor Vehicles," 72 *Federal Register* 69934, December 10, 2007.

[30] These statements are based on interviews with seven senior EPA staff, conducted by the House Oversight and Government Reform Committee, as reported in a letter from Hon. Henry A. Waxman, Chairman of the Committee, to EPA Administrator Stephen L. Johnson, March 12, 2008. The Administrator has not contradicted these statements.

[31] See [http://www.epa.gov/climatechange/emissions/downloads/ANPRPreamble.pdf].

[32] Ibid., pp. 7-8.

expressed substantial interest in this issue, which has been addressed in several oversight hearings and in a continuing investigation. The courts also continue to have a role: Massachusetts and other parties have petitioned the D.C. Circuit to order EPA to issue an endangerment decision within 60 days. Senator Feinstein's S. 2806 would do the same, requiring the Administrator to issue a finding within 60 days of the bill's enactment.

Other Clean Air Issues

In addition to climate change, there are a number of clean air issues in which Congress has expressed an interest. The rest of this report discusses seven of these issues, some of which have been the subject of oversight hearings.

Background

Despite steady improvements in air quality in many of the United States' most polluted cities, the goal of clean air continues to elude many areas. The most widespread problems involve ozone and fine particles. As of June 2008, 132 million people lived in areas classified "nonattainment" for the ozone National Ambient Air Quality Standard;[33] 88 million lived in areas that were nonattainment for fine particles ($PM_{2.5}$).[34]

Air quality has improved substantially since the passage of the Clean Air Act in 1970: annual emissions of the six most widespread ("criteria") air pollutants have declined 160 million tons (53%), despite major increases in population, motor vehicle miles traveled, and economic activity.[35]

Meanwhile, however, scientific understanding of the health effects of air pollution has caused the EPA to tighten standards for ozone and fine particles. (Fine particles, as defined by the EPA, consist of particulate matter 2.5 micrometers or less in diameter, abbreviated as $PM_{2.5}$.) The agency attributes at least 33,000 premature deaths and millions of lost work days annually to exceedances of the $PM_{2.5}$ standard. Recent research has tied ozone pollution to premature mortality as well. Thus, there is continuing pressure to tighten air quality standards: a tightening of the standard for fine particles was promulgated October 17, 2006. The ozone standards were strengthened March 12, 2008. In addition to the standards themselves, attention has focused on the major sources of ozone and particulate pollution, such as coal-fired power plants and mobile sources.

---

[33] Data for ozone nonattainment areas are from the U.S. EPA "Green Book," at [http://www.epa.gov/oar/oaqps/greenbk/gntc.html].

[34] Data for $PM_{2.5}$ nonattainment areas are also from the U.S. EPA "Green Book," at [http://www.epa.gov/oar/oaqps/greenbk/qntc.html].

[35] See U.S. EPA, "Air Emission Trends — Continued Progress Through 2005," at [http://www.epa.gov/airtrends/econ-emissions.html].

With this background in mind, the remainder of this report provides a discussion of several interrelated air issues of interest in the 110th Congress, including revision of the ozone, particulate, and lead standards, the role of independent scientific review in the setting of air quality standards, multi-pollutant legislation and the Clean Air Interstate Rule (CAIR) for electric power plants, mercury from power plants, and New Source Review. This report provides an overview of these issues; CRS reports that contain additional information and detailed sources are referenced in the appropriate sections.

Revision of the Ozone and Particulate Standards

Ozone NAAQS. EPA Administrator Stephen Johnson signed final changes to the National Ambient Air Quality Standard (NAAQS) for ozone on March 12, 2008; the proposal appeared in the *Federal Register* on March 27.[36] NAAQS are standards for outdoor (ambient) air that are intended to protect public health and welfare from harmful concentrations of pollution. By changing the standard, EPA has concluded that protecting public health and welfare requires lower concentrations of ozone pollution than it previously judged to be safe.

The ozone standard affects a larger percentage of the population than any other NAAQS: about 45% of the U.S. population currently lives in ozone "nonattainment" areas (the term EPA uses for areas that violate the standard), 132 million people in all. As a result of the standard's strengthening, more areas will be affected, and those already considered nonattainment may have to impose more stringent emission controls.

The revision lowers the primary (health-based) and secondary (welfare-based) standards from 0.08 parts per million (ppm) averaged over 8 hours to 0.075 ppm averaged over the same time. Using the most recent three years of monitoring data, 345 counties (54% of all counties with ozone monitors) would violate the new standards. Only 85 counties exceeded the pre-existing standards. Thus, the change in standards will have widespread impacts in areas across the country.

The revision follows a multi-year review of the science regarding ozone's effects on public health and welfare. The review found evidence of health effects, including mortality, at levels of exposure below the previous standard. As a result, both EPA staff and EPA's independent Clean Air Scientific Advisory Committee (CASAC) recommended strengthening it.[37] CASAC concluded, "There is no scientific justification for retaining the current primary 8-hr NAAQS...."[38] CASAC's

---

[36] 73 FR 16436.

[37] A fact sheet outlining EPA staff recommendations can be found at [http://www.epa.gov/ttn/naaqs/standards/ozone/data/2007_01_finalsp_factsheet.pdf]. The Clean Air Act Scientific Advisory Committee (CASAC) recommendations are at [http://yosemite.epa.gov/sab/sabproduct.nsf/FE915E916333D776852572AC007397B5/$File/casac-07-002.pdf].

[38] Letter of Dr. Rogene Henderson, Chair, CASAC, to Hon. Stephen L. Johnson, Administrator, U.S. EPA, October 24, 2006, p. 1, at [http://yosemite.epa.gov/sab/sabproduct.nsf/FE915E916333D776852572AC007397B5/$File/casac-07-002.pdf].

22-member panel unanimously recommended a range of 0.060 to 0.070 ppm for the primary (health-based) 8-hour standard.

The new standards will set in motion a long and complicated implementation process that has far-reaching impacts for public health, for sources of pollution in numerous economic sectors, and for state and local governments. The first step, designation of nonattainment areas, will not take place until 2010 at the earliest, but areas that exceed the new standards (based on current monitoring data) are already expressing concern about the potential impacts.

A number of issues arise as a result of the standards' adoption, including whether the Administrator's choices for the primary and secondary standards are backed by the available science. Not only are the Administrator's choices weaker than those proposed by CASAC, but the administrative record makes clear that, in part, they were dictated by the White House over the objections of EPA.

Whether the standards should lead to stronger federal controls on the sources of ozone pollution precursors is another likely issue. Current federal standards for cars, trucks, power plants, and other pollution sources are not strong enough to bring all areas into attainment, thus requiring local pollution control measures in many cases.

EPA, the states, and Congress may also wish to consider whether the current monitoring network is adequate to detect violations of a more stringent standard. Only 639 of the nation's 3,000 counties have ozone monitors in place. With half of those monitors showing violations of the new standards, questions arise as to air quality in unmonitored counties.

The Clean Air and Nuclear Safety subcommittee of the Senate Environment and Public Works Committee held a hearing on proposed changes to the standards, July 11, 2007. Additional hearings are expected now that the changes have been promulgated. For additional information on the ozone NAAQS proposal, see CRS Report RL34057, *Ozone Air Quality Standards: EPA's March 2008 Revision,* by James E. McCarthy.

Particulate Matter (PM) NAAQS. The ozone review followed closely on the heels of a revision to the NAAQS for particulate matter. EPA Administrator Stephen Johnson signed those revisions on September 21, 2006, and the standards appeared in the *Federal Register* on October 17, 2006.[39] In arriving at these revisions, EPA reviewed 2,000 scientific studies on particulates and found associations between particulates and numerous significant health problems, including aggravated asthma, chronic bronchitis, reduced lung function, irregular heart beat, heart attacks, and premature death in people with heart or lung disease.

The revisions strengthened the preexisting standard for $PM_{2.5}$, but the standard was not strengthened to the degree recommended by the agency's staff or scientific

---

[39] 71 *Federal Register* 61144. Extensive information related to the standards, including an eight-page fact sheet and maps and charts with background material, is available at [http://epa.gov/pm/actions.html].

advisors. As shown in **Table 1**, the new standard cuts the allowable concentration of $PM_{2.5}$ in the air averaged over 24-hour periods from 65 micrograms per cubic meter ($\mu g/m^3$) to 35 $\mu g/m^3$; the annual standard, set at 15 $\mu g/m^3$, does not change.

Table 1. Preexisting, Recommended, and New NAAQS for $PM_{2.5}$

	Annual Standard	**24-Hour Standard**
Preexisting Standards[a]	15 $\mu g/m^3$	65 $\mu g/m^3$
EPA Staff Recommendation	15 $\mu g/m^3$ and mid to lower end of 25-35 $\mu g/m^3$ OR 12-14 $\mu g/m^3$ and mid to lower end of 30-40 $\mu g/m^3$	
CASAC Recommendation	13 to 14 $\mu g/m^3$	30 to 35 $\mu g/m^3$
Administrator's Decision	15 $\mu g/m^3$	35 $\mu g/m^3$

a. Although these standards were promulgated in 1997, they are only now coming into effect, because of legal challenges, the need to establish a monitoring network, and various administrative factors. For additional information on implementation of the current standard, see CRS Report RL32431, *Particulate Matter (PM2.5): National Ambient Air Quality Standards (NAAQS)*, by Robert Esworthy.

EPA's professional staff and CASAC had recommended more stringent standards. CASAC endorsed a 24-hour standard in the range of 30 to 35 $\mu g/m^3$ and an annual standard in the range of 13 to 14 $\mu g/m^3$. Of the 22 CASAC panel members, 20 concurred in the recommendation.[40]

In the Administrator's judgment, the science underlying this recommendation was not sufficient, relying primarily on two studies, neither of which "provide[s] a clear basis for selecting a level lower than the current standard...."[41] The Administrator agrees with CASAC that the science shows a relationship between higher levels of $PM_{2.5}$ and an array of adverse health effects, but he believes there is too much uncertainty in the analysis to justify lowering the annual standard.[42] He also noted that EPA is undertaking substantial research to clarify which aspects of PM-related pollution are responsible for elevated risks of mortality and morbidity, including a multi-million-dollar research program whose timeline should permit the results to inform the Agency's next periodic reevaluation of the $PM_{2.5}$ standard, required by statute within five years. Thus, he concluded, "it would be wiser to

---

[40] By statute, CASAC consists of seven members chosen by the EPA Administrator. To review the NAAQS for a specific pollutant, CASAC forms a panel that includes as many subject experts as CASAC deems appropriate, in addition to the seven statutory CASAC members. Thus, the PM panel had 22 members.

[41] U.S. EPA, National Ambient Air Quality Standards for Particulate Matter, Proposed Rule, Preamble, 71 *Federal Register* 2651, January 17, 2006.

[42] See discussion beginning at 71 *Federal Register* 61172, October 17, 2006.

consider modification of the annual standard with a fuller body of information in hand than initiate a change in the annual standard at this time."[43]

The PM NAAQS also addresses slightly larger, but still inhalable, particles in the range of 10 to 2.5 micrometers. These are referred to as *thoracic coarse particles*, or $PM_{10\text{-}2.5}$. In its last review of the particulate standards (in 1997), the EPA had regulated these as particles 10 microns or smaller (PM_{10}), a category that overlapped the $PM_{2.5}$ category. Challenged in the D.C. Circuit Court of Appeals, the PM_{10} standard was remanded to the EPA, the court having concluded that PM_{10} is a "poorly matched indicator" for thoracic coarse particles because it includes the smaller $PM_{2.5}$ category as well as the larger particles. In response, in January 2006, the EPA proposed a 24-hour standard for $PM_{10\text{-}2.5}$. The standard would have been set at a level of 70 $\mu g/m^3$, compared with the current 24-hour PM_{10} standard of 150 $\mu g/m^3$. The final standards promulgated in October reversed course, leaving in place both the form of the standard (i.e., PM_{10}) and the 24-hour level (150 $\mu g/m^3$). The only change to the PM_{10} standard was the revocation of its *annual* component. The agency argues that it has provided more thorough reasoning in support of the use of PM_{10} as its coarse particle indicator, and believes that its explanation will satisfy the court.

CASAC's Views. The Administrator's decisions on particulate matter represented the first time in CASAC's nearly 30-year history that the promulgated standards fell outside of the range of the scientific panel's recommendations. (The ozone standard promulgated in March 2008 now provides a second instance.) In a letter dated September 29, 2006, the seven members of CASAC objected to the Administrator's actions, both as regards PM_{10} and $PM_{2.5}$. With regard to $PM_{2.5}$, the letter stated: "CASAC is concerned that EPA did not accept our finding that the annual $PM_{2.5}$ standard was not protective of human health and did not follow our recommendation for a change in that standard."[44] The letter noted that "there is clear and convincing scientific evidence that significant adverse human-health effects occur in response to short-term and chronic particulate matter exposures at and below 15 $\mu g/m^3$," and noted that 20 of the 22 Particulate Matter Review Panel members, including all 7 members of the statutory committee, were in "complete agreement" regarding the recommended reduction: "It is the CASAC's consensus scientific opinion that the decision to retain without change the annual $PM_{2.5}$ standard does not provide an 'adequate margin of safety ... requisite to protect the public health' (as required by the Clean Air Act)...."[45]

With regard to PM_{10}, the letter stated that CASAC was "completely surprised" at the decision to revert to the use of PM_{10} as the indicator for coarse particles, noting that the option of retaining the existing daily PM_{10} standard was not discussed during the advisory process and that CASAC views this decision as "highly problematic."

---

[43] 71 *Federal Register* 2652, January 17, 2006.

[44] Letter of Rogene Henderson et al. to Hon. Stephen L. Johnson, EPA Administrator, September 29, 2006, available at [http://www.epa.gov/sab/pdf/casac-ltr-06-003.pdf].

[45] Ibid. Italics in original.

The Administrator is not required by statute to follow CASAC's recommendations; the act (Section 307(d)(3)) requires only that the Administrator set forth any pertinent findings, recommendations, and comments by CASAC (and the National Academy of Sciences) and, if his proposal differs in an important respect from any of their recommendations, provide an explanation of the reasons for such differences. Courts, in reviewing EPA regulations, generally defer to the Administrator's judgment on scientific matters, focusing more on issues of procedure, jurisdiction, and standing. Nevertheless, CASAC's detailed objections to the Administrator's decisions and its description of the process as having failed to meet statutory and procedural requirements could play a role during judicial review.[46]

Implementation of the PM NAAQS. A NAAQS does not directly limit emissions; rather, it represents the EPA Administrator's formal judgment regarding the level of ambient pollution that will protect public health with an adequate margin of safety. Promulgation of NAAQS sets in motion a process under which states and the EPA first identify nonattainment areas. After these areas are formally designated (a process the EPA estimates will take until April 2010 for the revised $PM_{2.5}$ standard), the states have three years to submit State Implementation Plans (SIPs) that identify specific regulations and emission control requirements that will bring the area into attainment. Attainment of the revised standard is to be achieved by 2015, according to the EPA, with a possible extension to 2020.

(For a more detailed discussion of the PM NAAQS, see CRS Report RL33254, *Air Quality: EPA's 2006 Changes to the Particulate Matter (PM) Standard*, by Robert Esworthy and James E. McCarthy.)

CASAC's Role in the NAAQS-Setting Process

The completion of the PM NAAQS review was followed by an EPA announcement, on December 7, 2006, that it will modify the process for setting and reviewing NAAQS. Sections 108 and 109 of the Clean Air Act establish statutory requirements for the identification of NAAQS (or "criteria") air pollutants[47] and the setting and periodic review of the NAAQS standards. However, the process used by the agency is as much the result of 37 years of agency practice as it is of statutory requirements. In Section 109, for example, the statute establishes a Clean Air Scientific Advisory Committee to make recommendations to the Administrator regarding new NAAQS and, at five-year intervals, to make reviews of existing NAAQS with recommendations for revisions. In practice, EPA staff, not CASAC, have prepared these reviews, drafting "criteria documents," which review the science and health effects of criteria air pollutants, and "staff papers," which make policy recommendations. CASAC's role has been to review and approve these EPA

---

[46] The standards have been challenged by 13 states, a large number of industry and environmental groups, and others. The case is American Farm Bureau Federation v. U.S. EPA, no. 06-1410 (D.C. Cir).

[47] Criteria pollutants are pollutants that endanger public health or welfare, in the Administrator's judgment, and whose presence in ambient air results from numerous or diverse sources.

documents before they went to the agency's political appointees and the Administrator for final decisions.

Under the new procedures, the EPA's political appointees will have a role early in the process, helping to choose the scientific studies to be reviewed, and CASAC will no longer have a role in approving the policy staff paper with its recommendations to the Administrator. CASAC will be relegated to commenting on the policy paper after it appears in the *Federal Register*, during a public comment period. The goal, according to agency officials, is to speed up the review process, which has consistently taken longer than the five years allowed by statute. "These improvements will help the agency meet the goal of reviewing each NAAQS on a five-year cycle as required by the Clean Air Act, without compromising the scientific integrity of the process,"[48] according to the memorandum that finalized the changes. The changes concern environmental groups and some in the scientific community, however, because they appear to give a larger role to the agency's political appointees and a smaller role to EPA staff and CASAC.

Although the new NAAQS review procedures will change the role that CASAC has historically played, CASAC, at first, appeared less concerned with the changes than some who have advocated on its behalf. When the December 2006 decision memorandum was released, the committee's Chair said CASAC did not plan to issue a formal response. In response to a draft of the changes, the committee had made a number of suggestions, some of which, such as the convening of a science workshop at the outset of the process to better focus the review, were incorporated into the decision memorandum. The memorandum also addressed another of CASAC's major concerns, that the old process spent too much time compiling an encyclopedic review of the literature, much of which had little relevance to the policy questions that needed to be addressed. With respect to EPA taking comments from CASAC at the same time that it considers comments from the public, CASAC's Chair was reported to say, "[S]ome of the members were concerned but most are not, because it doesn't change CASAC's ability to comment."[49]

In early February 2007, however, reports circulated that CASAC had changed its mind. After its first experience with the new NAAQS review process (at a meeting to consider the NAAQS for lead),[50] it was reported that the committee would compose a letter to the EPA Administrator critical of the new process:

---

[48] "Process for Reviewing National Ambient Air Quality Standards," Memorandum of Marcus Peacock, Deputy EPA Administrator, to Dr. George Gray, Assistant Administrator, Office of Research and Development, and Bill Wehrum, Acting Assistant Administrator, Office of Air and Radiation, December 7, 2006, p. 3, at [http://www.epa.gov/ttn/naaqs/memo_process_for_reviewing_naaqs.pdf].

[49] Comment of Dr. Rogene Henderson, CASAC Chair, in "EPA Adviser Plays Down Democrats' Criticism over New NAAQS Changes," *Inside EPA Clean Air Report*, December 14, 2006.

[50] A CASAC Review Panel met to consider the Lead NAAQS on February 6-7, 2007.

Henderson [CASAC Chair, Dr. Rogene Henderson] said that when EPA first proposed the NAAQS process changes in response to a memo by Deputy Administrator Marcus Peacock, CASAC had "misunderstood how it would be implemented."

However, "the full consequences became apparent in the lead meeting," she said, with panel members concerned about not being able to review staff recommendations. The new process "does not allow CASAC time for appropriate input to evaluate the science," she said.[51]

Negotiations between CASAC and EPA management followed the February 2007 public meeting, with the result that EPA modified its schedule to allow the CASAC Lead Review Panel to review a second draft of EPA's risk and exposure assessment before the agency's Policy Assessment was published in the *Federal Register*. This appeared to mollify some of CASAC's concerns, but CASAC continued to express "serious concerns" about other aspects of the Lead NAAQS review.[52]

Reaction elsewhere has been stronger. Responding to the changes at the time of their announcement, the incoming Chair of the Environment and Public Works Committee, Senator Barbara Boxer, called them "unacceptable," and said the committee planned to make them a top priority for oversight in the 110th Congress.[53] (The committee included them among the topics it considered February 6, 2007, in a hearing on "Oversight of Recent EPA Decisions.") Seven Democratic members of the committee, including Senator Boxer, wrote EPA Administrator Johnson, December 21, 2006, to express their strong opposition to the changes and to ask him to "abandon" them.[54] Thus, the role of CASAC in NAAQS reviews could be the subject of further scrutiny in Congress.

---

[51] "Advisory Panel to Recommend Stricter Limit for Agency's Air Quality Standard for Lead," *Daily Environment Report*, February 9, 2007, p. A-1.

[52] See letter of Dr. Rogene Henderson, Chair, CASAC, to Hon. Stephen L. Johnson, Administrator, U.S. EPA, March 27, 2007, at [http://yosemite.epa.gov/sab/sabproduct.nsf/4620a620d0120f93852572410080d786/989B57DCD436111B852572AC0079DA8A/$File/casac-07-003.pdf]. CASAC reiterated concerns about the new process in January 2008, based on their experience with the review of the lead NAAQS, discussed in the next section of this report. See letter of Dr. Rogene Henderson, Chair, CASAC, et al., to Hon. Stephen L. Johnson, Administrator, U.S. EPA, January 23, 2008, at [http://yosemite.epa.gov/sab/sabproduct.nsf/WebCASAC/B7E63138A2041A22852573DB005D4E98/$File/EPA-CASAC-08-008-unsigned.pdf].

[53] Office of Senator Barbara Boxer, "Boxer Statement on EPA's Politicization of Clean Air Health Standards," Press Release, December 8, 2006, at [http://boxer.senate.gov/news/releases/record.cfm?id=266781].

[54] Office of Senator Barbara Boxer, "Democratic Members of Senate EPW Committee Warn EPA on Air Rollbacks," Press Release, December 21, 2006, at [http://boxer.senate.gov/news/releases/record.cfm?id=267092].

Revision of the NAAQS for Lead

As a result of a suit filed by the Missouri Coalition for the Environment and others in May 2004,[55] EPA is under court order to complete a review of the NAAQS for lead by October 15, 2008. On May 1, 2008, the agency proposed a revision that would strengthen the NAAQS, reducing it from 1.5 micrograms of lead per cubic meter ($\mu g/m^3$) to within the range of 0.10 to 0.30 $\mu g/m^3$. The proposal's publication in the *Federal Register* began a public comment period that runs through August 4, with public hearings in St. Louis and Baltimore.

Regulation of Lead: A Success, But Not Based on NAAQS. The current lead NAAQS was promulgated in 1978. The Clean Air Act requires that NAAQS be reviewed every five years, but a review of the standard has not been completed since that time.[56] Despite this, regulation of airborne lead is often described as one of the key successes of the Clean Air Act and of the Environmental Protection Agency. The success occurred largely because EPA and other federal agencies used authorities other than NAAQS to order the removal of lead from a wide variety of products.

In 1970, lead was widely used as a gasoline additive, and emissions of lead nationwide totaled 224,100 tons. Lead was also present then in many consumer products, and thus was emitted to the air in industrial processes and from waste incinerators. The phasing out of lead from gasoline, paint, packaging materials, and consumer products, as well as stricter controls on industrial emissions, reduced lead emissions 98%, to 4,228 tons in 2000.

As a result, there are now only two nonattainment areas for lead under the 1978 standard: East Helena, MT, and Herculaneum, MO, with a combined population of 4,664 people. Both of these towns were sites of lead smelters that operated for more than 100 years, contaminating air, water, and soil nearby.

Most of these reductions were motivated by concerns other than the effects of lead concentrations in ambient air. Lead was removed from gasoline in large part because it ruined the catalytic converters placed on vehicle exhaust systems, which were needed to control smog. Lead was removed from paint primarily to avoid its ingestion by children.

The Basis for the Proposed Standard. Airborne lead continues to cause negative effects, despite the reduction in emissions. In the current NAAQS review, EPA identified more than 6,000 studies on lead health effects, environmental effects, and lead in the air published since the previous review. These studies have found evidence of health effects at the levels of exposure currently experienced by much of the U.S. population. Lead particles can be inhaled or ingested, and, once in the body,

---

[55] Missouri Coalition for the Environment v. U.S. EPA, 2005 WL 2234579 (E.D. Mo. September 14, 2005).

[56] EPA began a lead NAAQS review and issued a Criteria Document in 1986 and a Staff Paper in 1990, but the agency never completed the review: i.e., there was no final decision published in the *Federal Register*.

can cause lower IQ and effects on learning, memory, and behavior in children. In adults, lead exposure is linked to increased blood pressure, cardiovascular disease, and decreased kidney function.

Thus, EPA staff and CASAC, the independent panel of scientists who advise the EPA Administrator, concluded that the NAAQS established in 1978 is far too lenient, that lead in ambient air still poses a threat to public health, and that the NAAQS should be significantly strengthened. CASAC and EPA staff recommended that the standard be reduced from 1.5 $\mu g/m^3$ to no higher than 0.2 $\mu g/m^3$. In proposing a more stringent NAAQS, the Administrator sided with the scientists, rejecting arguments that a NAAQS is no longer needed and concluding that the NAAQS needed to be substantially strengthened; but his proposed range is, in part, not as stringent as the scientists recommended.

The Administrator's decision regarding the proposed range appears to rest, in part, on a potentially controversial interpretation of the statutory requirement to "protect ... public health" with "an adequate margin of safety." The preamble to the proposed rule states that CASAC and the American Academy of Pediatrics both advised the agency that mean IQ loss within a range of 1 to 2 points "could be significant from a public health perspective." But the Administrator decided that a standard level should be selected to provide protection from air-related IQ loss *in excess of* this range (emphasis added).[57] In other words, the Administrator's interpretation of protecting public health with an adequate margin of safety was to choose a standard that would likely result in an IQ loss that his scientific advisers told him could be significant from a public health perspective.[58]

The degree to which these arguments prove controversial is likely to depend on where in the proposed range the Administrator sets the final standard. If his choice falls within the lower half (0.10 to 0.20 $\mu g/m^3$), there would be less ground for challenge. A standard in that portion of the range would be supported by EPA staff's conclusions based on their review of the 6,000 scientific studies, and would be supported by the unanimous conclusions of the 23-member CASAC review panel. If his choice falls in the upper half of the range (0.21 to 0.30 $\mu g/m^3$), or higher, it would lack this support and would almost certainly join other recent EPA decisions in being challenged in the U.S. Court of Appeals for the D.C. Circuit.

---

[57] U.S. EPA, National Ambient Air Quality Standards for Lead, Proposed Rule (pre-publication copy), at [http://www.epa.gov/air/lead/pdfs/20080501_proposal_fr.pdf], p. 235.

[58] The exact words of the preamble are: "... the Administrator first notes that ideally air-related (as well as other) exposures to environmental Pb [lead] would be reduced to the point that no IQ impact in children would occur. The Administrator recognizes, however, that in the case of setting a NAAQS, he is required to make a judgment as to what degree of protection is requisite to protect public health with an adequate margin of safety. ... Considering the advice of CASAC and public comments on this issue, notably including the comments of the American Academy of Pediatrics, the Administrator proposes to conclude that an air-related population mean IQ loss within the range of 1 to 2 points could be significant from a public health perspective, and that a standard level should be selected to provide protection from air-related population mean IQ loss in excess of this range." Ibid.

Implementing a Revised Standard. Assuming a new standard is promulgated in October, nonattainment areas will have to be identified (not expected to occur until October 2011), following which there will be a 5- to 10-year-long implementation process in which states and local governments will identify and implement measures to reduce lead in the air.

Lead Monitoring. Besides finding that the 1978 NAAQS is inadequate to protect public health and welfare, EPA's review concluded that "[t]he current monitoring network is inadequate to assess national compliance with the proposed revised lead standards."[59] Only 104 of the roughly 3,000 counties in the United States (about 3%) currently have lead monitors, leaving many areas of the country without any means of determining whether they are in violation of the lead NAAQS. In fact, according to EPA's Office of Air Quality Planning and Standards, at least 24 states have no monitors at all.[60]

To address this shortfall, EPA proposes to require monitors near all sources of lead that exceed an emissions threshold of between 200 and 600 kilograms (441 to 1,323 pounds) per year. The final threshold would be determined by the stringency of the Administrator's final choice of a NAAQS — a more stringent NAAQS would be tied to a monitoring requirement that includes areas with smaller sources.

EPA also proposes to require a small network of monitors to be placed in urban areas with populations greater than one million to gather information on the general population's exposure to lead in the air. (For additional information, see CRS Report RL34479, *Revising the National Ambient Air Quality Standard for Lead*.)

CAIR and Multi-Pollutant Legislation for Power Plants

Besides air quality standards, the major focus of interest among members of Congress and other policy makers concerned with air quality in recent years has been the regulation of electric power plants. The centerpiece of the Bush Administration's approach to regulating power plants has been the Clean Air Interstate Rule (CAIR), a cap-and-trade regulation designed to reduce emissions of sulfur dioxide and nitrogen oxides, reducing the downwind effects of these pollutants on attainment of the ozone and $PM_{2.5}$ air quality standards. CAIR was vacated by the U.S. Court of

---

[59] U.S. EPA, "May 2008 Proposal, National Ambient Air Quality Standards for Lead, General Overview," Text Slides, at [http://www.epa.gov/air/lead/pdfs/20080501_text1.pdf], p. 17.

[60] Several of the states without monitors have large sources of lead emissions. Arkansas, for example, has two of the 12 largest stationary sources of lead in the United States (those with lead emissions exceeding 5 tons per year), but, according to EPA, no ambient lead monitors. Similarly, large sources in Oklahoma, the Texas panhandle, and other locations appear to be located more than 100 miles from the nearest ambient monitor. Montana has one of only two nonattainment areas for the 1978 lead standard, but, according to EPA, it has no ambient lead monitors. Data on monitor locations was provided by EPA's Office of Air Quality Planning and Standards, May 6, 2008. See also "EPA to Seek Comment on Increasing Air Monitors as Part of Lead Rulemaking," *Daily Environment Report*, November 29, 2007, p. A-10.

Appeals for the D.C. Circuit July 11, 2008, in *North Carolina v. EPA*,[61] dealing a serious setback to the Administration's approach to controlling power plant pollution.

Coal-fired power plants are among the largest sources of air pollution in the United States; however, under the Clean Air Act, they are not necessarily subject to stringent requirements. Emissions and the required control equipment can vary depending on the location of the plant, when it was constructed, whether it has undergone major modifications, the specific type of fuel it burns, and, to some extent, the vagaries of EPA enforcement policies. More than half a dozen separate Clean Air Act programs could potentially be used to control emissions, which makes compliance strategy complicated for utilities and difficult for regulators. Because the cost of the most stringent available controls, for the entire industry, could range into the tens of billions of dollars, utilities have fought hard and rather successfully to limit or delay regulations affecting them, particularly with respect to plants constructed before the Clean Air Act of 1970 was passed.

As a result, emissions from power plants have not been reduced as much as those from some other sources. Many plants built in the 1950s and 1960s (generally referred to as "grandfathered" plants) have little emission control equipment. Collectively, these plants are large sources of pollution. In 2003, power plants accounted for 10.2 million tons of sulfur dioxide (SO_2) emissions (70% of the U.S. total), about 45 tons of mercury emissions (more than 40% of the U.S. total), and 3.6 million tons of nitrogen oxides (19% of the U.S. total). Power plants are also considered major sources of fine particles ($PM_{2.5}$), many of which form in the atmosphere from emissions from a wide range of stationary and mobile sources. In addition, power plants account for about 40% of U.S. anthropogenic emissions of the greenhouse gas carbon dioxide; these emissions are not subject to federal regulation but have been the focus of much debate in recent years.

With new ambient air quality standards for ozone and fine particles taking effect, emissions of NOx (which contributes to the formation of ozone and fine particles) and SO_2 (which is also among the sources of fine particles) would necessarily have to be reduced to meet standards. Mercury emissions have also been a focus of concern: 48 states have issued fish consumption advisories due to mercury pollution, covering 14 million acres of lakes, 882,000 river miles, and the coastal waters of 13 entire states. The continuing controversy over the interpretation of New Source Review requirements for existing power plants (discussed below) is also exerting pressure for a more predictable regulatory structure.

Thus, many in industry, environmental groups, Congress, and the Administration have said, for several years now, that the time is ripe for legislation that addresses power plant pollution in a comprehensive (multi-pollutant) fashion. Such legislation (the Administration version of which was entitled the Clear Skies Act)[62] would address the major pollutants on a coordinated schedule and would rely,

---

[61] No. 05-1244, 2008 WL 2698180 (D.C. Cir. July 11, 2008).

[62] The Administration first proposed the Clear Skies Act on February 14, 2002, and the bill was introduced by request in the 107th Congress as H.R. 5266/S. 2815. In the 109th

(continued...)

to a large extent, on a system such as the one used in the acid rain program, where national or regional caps on emissions are implemented through a system of tradeable allowances. The key questions have been how stringent the caps should be and whether carbon dioxide (CO_2), the major gas of concern with regard to climate change, would be among the emissions subject to a cap.

It now seems unlikely that the 110th Congress will take action regarding multi-pollutant legislation. Four bills have been introduced in the Senate and one in the House — S. 1168, S. 1177, S. 1201, S. 1554, and H.R. 3989 — but no action has been scheduled, and little time remains. The focus of power plant regulation seems to have shifted toward broader climate change bills, which are now also seen as unlikely to pass in this Congress.

Clean Air Interstate Rule (CAIR). The Senate Environment and Public Works Committee has voted twice on a multi-pollutant bill, but none of the bills has progressed to the House or Senate floor. On March 10, 2005, however, EPA announced that it would use existing Clean Air Act authority to promulgate final regulations similar to the Administration's multi-pollutant bill (the "Clear Skies" bill) for utility emissions of SO_2 and NOx in 28 eastern states and the District of Columbia.[63] The Clean Air Interstate Rule (CAIR) established cap-and-trade provisions that mimicked those of Clear Skies, but the regulations covered only the eastern half of the country, and, as a regulation, CAIR had no authority to allow the EPA to remove existing Clean Air Act requirements, as Clear Skies would have done. Under CAIR, the EPA projected that nationwide emissions of SO_2 would decline 53% by 2015 and NOx emissions 48%. The agency also projected that the rule would result in $85-$100 billion in health benefits annually by 2015, including the prevention of 17,000 premature deaths annually.[64] CAIR's health and environmental benefits would be more than 25 times greater than its costs, according to the EPA.[65]

CAIR was one of the few Bush Administration environmental initiatives that was generally supported by environmentalists. It also had broad support among the regulated community. But a variety of petitioners, including the State of North Carolina, which argued that the rule was not strong enough to address pollution from upwind sources, and some individual utilities that felt they were unfairly treated by the rule's emission budgets, challenged the rule in the D.C. Circuit, and the court vacated it July 11, 2008. A unanimous court found, in general, that EPA lacked authority to promulgate a regional cap-and-trade rule under Section 110 of the Clean Air Act unless it could show a link between the pollution emitted in specific states

---

[62] (...continued)
Congress, a somewhat modified Clear Skies bill was introduced as S. 131. Clear Skies has not been introduced in the 110th Congress.

[63] The rule appeared in the *Federal Register* on May 12, 2005 (70 FR 25162).

[64] U.S. EPA, Office of Air and Radiation, "Clean Air Interstate Rule — Basic Information," available at [http://www.epa.gov/interstateairquality/basic.html].

[65] Similarly, any of the multi-pollutant bills would be expected to have benefits far outweighing their costs.

and nonattainment of standards or failure to maintain standards in downwind states. The court found that EPA had established a significant contribution made by power plants to pollution levels in other states as required by Section 110, but that its methodology for establishing emission budgets was unrelated to that link. The court also found the fuel adjustment factors in the rule to be arbitrary and capricious. It concluded "CAIR's flaws are deep. No amount of tinkering will transform CAIR, as written, into an acceptable rule."[66]

From a policy standpoint, the court's decision seriously undermines the Bush Administration approach to clean air over the past eight years. CAIR was the lynchpin that held together the Administration's strategy for attainment of the ozone and fine particulate National Ambient Air Quality Standards (NAAQS), for achieving reductions in mercury emissions from coal-fired powerplants (as discussed further below), for addressing regional haze impacts from powerplants, and for responding to state petitions to control upwind sources of ozone and fine particulate pollution under Section 126 of the Clean Air Act. (For additional information on the CAIR rule, see CRS Report RL34589, *Clean Air After the CAIR Decision: Back to Square one?*, by James E. McCarthy, Larry B. Parker, and Robert Meltz; and CRS Report RL32927, *Clean Air Interstate Rule: Review and Analysis*, by Larry Parker. For a discussion of the costs and benefits of the principal multi-pollutant approaches, see CRS Report RL33165, *Costs and Benefits of Clear Skies: EPA's Analysis of Multi-Pollutant Clean Air Bills*, by James E. McCarthy and Larry B. Parker.)

Mercury from Power Plants

At the same time that EPA promulgated CAIR, the agency finalized through regulation a cap-and-trade program for mercury emissions from electric utilities.[67] On February 8, 2008, the U.S. Court of Appeals for the D.C. Circuit vacated these regulations as well and remanded them to EPA for reconsideration.

Background. EPA was required by the terms of the 1990 Clean Air Act Amendments and a 1998 consent agreement to determine whether regulation of mercury from power plants under Section 112 of the Clean Air Act was appropriate and necessary. It concluded that it was, in a December 2000 regulatory finding. The finding added coal- and oil-fired electric generating units to the list of categories of sources of hazardous air pollutants, and triggered other provisions of the consent agreement: that the agency propose Maximum Achievable Control Technology (MACT) standards for them by December 15, 2003, and finalize the standards by March 15, 2005.

Rather than promulgate MACT standards, however, which would have required controls on each coal-fired power plant by 2008, EPA reversed its December 2000

---

[66] 2008 Westlaw 2698180, *30.

[67] The mercury rule appeared in the *Federal Register* in two parts: in the first part, on March 29, 2005, the agency revised its determination that mercury emissions from electric generating units should be regulated as hazardous air pollutants under Section 112 of the Clean Air Act (70 FR 15994); in the second part, on May 18, 2005, the agency promulgated a cap-and-trade program under Section 111 of the act (70 FR 28606).

finding in March 2005, and established through regulations a national cap-and-trade system for power plant emissions of mercury. The final cap would have been 15 tons of emissions nationwide in 2018 (about a 70% reduction from 1999 levels, when achieved). There would also have been an intermediate cap of 38 tons in 2010. This intermediate cap would not have actually limited emissions, however, since the agency projected emissions at 31 tons in 2010 even if 99% of the generating units installed no mercury control equipment.

The caps would have been implemented through an allowance system similar to that used in the acid rain and CAIR programs, through which utilities can either control the pollutant directly or purchase excess allowances from other plants that have instituted controls more stringently or sooner than required. As with the acid rain and CAIR programs, early reductions could have been banked for later use, which the agency said would result in utilities delaying compliance with the full 70% reduction until well beyond 2018, as they used up banked allowances rather than installing further controls. The agency's analysis projected actual emissions to be 24.3 tons (less than a 50% reduction) as late as 2020. Full compliance with the 70% reduction would have been delayed until after 2025.[68] (For additional information on the mercury rule, see CRS Report RL32868, *Mercury Emissions from Electric Power Plants: An Analysis of EPA's Cap-and-Trade Regulations*, by James E. McCarthy.)

The Court's Decision. The D.C. Circuit, in a 3-0 decision handed down February 8, 2008,[69] found that once the agency had listed electric generating units (EGUs) as a source of hazardous air pollutants, it had to proceed with MACT regulations under Section 112 of the act unless it "delisted" the source category, under procedures the act sets forth in Section 112(c)(9). Delisting would have required the agency to find that no EGU's emissions exceeded a level adequate to protect public health with an ample margin of safety, and that no adverse environmental effect would result from any source — a difficult test to meet, given the agency's estimate that EGUs are responsible for more than 40% of mercury emissions from all U.S. sources. Rather than delist the EGU source category, therefore, the agency maintained that it could simply reverse its December 2000 "appropriate and necessary" finding, a decision that was much simpler because there were no statutory criteria to meet. The court found this approach unlawful. "This explanation deploys the logic of the Queen of Hearts, substituting EPA's desires for the plain text of Section 112(c)(9)," the court said in its unanimous opinion.

Other Mercury Issues. Besides the question of whether EPA complied with the law's requirements, critics have found other flaws in EPA's cap-and-trade approach to controlling mercury. One of the main criticisms has been that it would not address "hot spots," areas where mercury emissions and/or concentrations in water bodies are greater than elsewhere. It would have allowed a facility to purchase allowances and avoid any emission controls, if that compliance approach made the

---

[68] U.S. EPA, Office of Air Quality Planning and Standards, *Regulatory Impact Analysis of the Clean Air Mercury Rule*, March 2005, Table 7-3, p. 7-5, at [http://www.epa.gov/ttn/atw/utility/ria_final.pdf].

[69] New Jersey v. EPA, 2008 Westlaw 341338.

most sense to the plant's owners and operators. If plants near hot spots did so, the cap-and-trade system might not have reduced mercury concentrations in the most contaminated areas. By contrast, a MACT standard would require reductions at all plants, and would therefore be expected to improve conditions at hot spots.

Many also argue that the mercury regulations should be more stringent or implemented more quickly than the cap-and-trade regulations would have required. To a large extent, these arguments, and EPA's counter-arguments, rest on assumptions concerning the availability of control technologies. Controlling SO_2, NOx, and mercury simultaneously, as the agency prefers, would allow utilities to maximize "co-benefits" of emission controls. Controls such as scrubbers and fabric filters, both of which are widely used today to control SO_2 and particulates, have the side effect of reducing mercury emissions to some extent. Under EPA's cap-and-trade regulations, both the 2010 and 2018 mercury emission standards were set to maximize use of these co-benefits, which would have resulted from controls installed to comply with CAIR. As a result, few controls would have been required to specifically address mercury emissions before the 2020s, the costs specific to controlling mercury would be minimal, and emissions would decline to about 50% of the 1999 level in 2020.

Besides citing the cost advantage of relying on co-benefits, EPA has claimed that technology specifically designed to control mercury emissions (such as activated carbon injection, ACI) would not be generally available until after 2010. This assertion has been widely disputed. ACI and fabric filters have been in use on municipal waste and medical waste incinerators for more than a decade, and have been successfully demonstrated in at least 16 full-scale tests at coal-fired power plants, for periods as long as a year. Manufacturers of pollution controls and many others maintain that if the agency required the use of ACI and fabric filters at power plants, reductions in mercury emissions as great as 90% could be achieved at reasonable cost in the near future. Relying on these assertions, about 20 states have promulgated requirements stricter than the federal program, with several requiring 80% to 90% mercury reductions before 2010. (For additional information, see CRS Report RL33535, *Mercury Emissions from Electric Power Plants: States Are Setting Stricter Limits*, by James E. McCarthy.)

Next Steps. Under the D.C. Circuit's ruling, unless EPA delists the power plant category, it would appear that the agency does not have the legislative authority to establish a cap-and-trade program for their mercury emissions: the agency appears to be required by the statute to impose MACT standards on each individual plant once it has listed the category. The agency can, of course, appeal the court's ruling: on March 24, the agency filed a petition for reconsideration by the full "en banc" Court of Appeals, which was denied by the court May 20, but it could still seek resolution by the Supreme Court. It will also require some deliberation and some time to develop MACT regulations if it is denied or loses an appeal. To speed this process, Senator Carper introduced S. 2643, which would require the Administrator to propose MACT standards no later than October 1, 2008, and would require new and existing power plants to achieve a reduction in mercury emissions of not less than 90%. The bill joins six earlier bills that would set deadlines and generally require reductions of at least 90%. (For additional information, see CRS Report

RS22817, *The D.C. Circuit Rejects EPA's Mercury Rules: New Jersey v. EPA*, by Robert Meltz and James E. McCarthy.)

In the meantime, while the agency considers its options and develops any new regulations in response to the remand, new coal-fired electric generating units and modifications of existing units will be required to obtain permits under a provisions of the law known as the "MACT hammer" (Section 112(g)(2)). Under this provision, if no applicable emission limits have been established, no person may construct a new major source or modify an existing major source in the category unless the Administrator or the state determine on a case-by-case basis that they meet the maximum achievable emission controls. On February 28, 2008, the Natural Resources Defense Council (NRDC) released a list of 32 coal-fired power plants in 13 states that it believes must now adopt MACT mercury controls under this provision.[70]

New Source Review

A related issue that has driven some of the debate over the regulation of power plant emissions is whether the EPA has adequately enforced existing regulations, using a process called New Source Review (NSR). The New Source Review debate has occurred largely in the courts. The EPA took a more aggressive stance on NSR under the Clinton Administration, filing lawsuits against 13 utilities for violations at 51 plants in 13 states. The Bush Administration has taken action against an additional half a dozen utilities and, after years of negotiation, has settled many of the original suits. In the meantime, however, it has proposed major changes in the NSR regulations that critics argue will weaken or eliminate New Source Review as it pertains to modifications of existing plants.

The controversy over the NSR process stems from the EPA's use of it to require the installation of best available pollution controls on existing stationary sources of air pollution that have been modified. The Clean Air Act requires that plants undergoing modifications meet these NSR requirements, but industry has often avoided the NSR process by claiming that changes to existing sources were "routine maintenance" rather than modifications. In the 1990s, the EPA began reviewing records of electric utilities, petroleum refineries, and other industries to determine whether the changes were, in fact, routine. As a result of these reviews, since late 1999, EPA and the Department of Justice have filed suit or administrative actions against numerous large sources of pollution, alleging that they made major modifications to their plants, extending plant life and increasing output, without undergoing required New Source Reviews and without installing best available pollution controls.

Of the utilities charged with NSR violations, at least 13 have settled with the EPA, generally without going to trial. Under the settlements, they have agreed to spend about $10 billion over the next decade on pollution controls or fuel switching

---

[70] NRDC, "32 Coal-Fired Power Plants in 13 States Now Up in the Air After Major Court Ruling on Mercury," Press Release, February 28, 2008, at [http://www.nrdc.org/media/2008/080228.asp].

to reduce emissions at their affected units. Combined, these companies will reduce pollution by 1.65 million tons annually. Since July 25, 2000, the agency has also reached 17 agreements with petroleum refiners representing three-fourths of industry capacity. The refiners agreed to settle potential charges of NSR violations by paying fines and installing equipment to eliminate 315,000 tons of pollution.

Those utilities charged with NSR violations that have not settled with the EPA claim that the EPA has reinvented the NSR rules, and that the agency's stricter interpretation of what constitutes routine maintenance will prevent them from making changes that would have previously been allowed without a commitment of time and money for permit reviews and the installation of expensive pollution control equipment. This provides disincentives for power producers, refiners, and others to expand output at existing facilities, they maintain.

The first case involving one of the nonsettling utilities went to trial in February 2003. In an August 7, 2003, decision, the U.S. District Court for the Southern District of Ohio found that Ohio Edison had violated the Clean Air Act 11 times in modifying its W. H. Sammis power plant. The company subsequently settled the case, agreeing to spend $1.1 billion to install controls that are expected to reduce pollution by 212,000 tons annually.[71] In a second case, decided in April 2004 but appealed all the way to the U.S. Supreme Court, Duke Energy was found not to have violated the act despite undertaking modifications that increased total emissions without undergoing New Source Review. The U.S. District Court for the Middle District of North Carolina, in a decision upheld by the Fourth Circuit Court of Appeals, held that since the maximum *hourly* emissions rate did not increase as a result of the modifications, even if annual emissions did increase, the company was not required to undergo NSR and install more stringent pollution controls.[72] On April 2, 2007, the Supreme Court overturned the lower court rulings in a unanimous decision, finding that EPA's regulations, promulgated in 1980, clearly specified an increase in actual annual emissions as the measure of whether a permit for a modification was required. To argue otherwise now would be to challenge the validity of the regulations, the Court concluded; such a challenge needs to be filed with the D.C. Circuit Court of Appeals within 60 days of a regulation's promulgation — it cannot be done more than 20 years later in the Fourth Circuit.[73]

While pursuing these enforcement actions, the Bush Administration has promulgated a number of changes to the NSR regulations that would make future enforcement of NSR less likely. In December 2002 and October 2003, the agency promulgated five sets of changes to the NSR rules. The most controversial were new regulations defining what constitutes routine maintenance.[74] The new regulations would have exempted industrial facilities from undergoing NSR (and thus from

---

[71] United States v. Ohio Edison Co., No. C-2-99-1181, [S.D. Ohio].

[72] United States v. Duke Energy Corp., 278 F.Supp. 2d 619 [M.D.N.C. 2003] affirmed, 411 F. 3d 539 [4th Cir., 2005], petition for cert. Filed [No. 05-848].

[73] The decision, Environmental Defense v. Duke Energy Corp., April 2, 2007, can be found at [http://www.supremecourtus.gov/opinions/06pdf/05-848.pdf].

[74] These changes appeared in the *Federal Register* on October 27, 2003 (68 FR 61247).

installing new emission controls) if they were replacing safety, reliability, and efficiency-rated components with new, functionally equivalent equipment, and if the cost of the replacement components was less than 20% of the replacement value of the process unit. Using this benchmark, few, if any, plant modifications would trigger new pollution controls.

These changes were highly controversial. The Administration and its supporters characterized them as streamlining or improving the program; others saw them as permanently "grandfathering" older, more polluting facilities from ever having to meet the clean air standards required of newer plants. Fifteen states, three municipalities, and several environmental groups filed suit to block the "equipment replacement / routine maintenance" rule. The rule was stayed by the U.S. Court of Appeals for the D.C. Circuit on December 24, 2003. On March 17, 2006, a three-judge panel of the court unanimously struck the rule down. In its decision, the court held that the EPA's attempt to change the NSR regulations was "contrary to the plain language" of the Clean Air Act.[75]

The EPA proposed further changes to the NSR regulations on October 20, 2005, and September 14, 2006[76]; these regulations have yet to be promulgated. Under the October 2005 proposal, power plants could modify existing facilities without triggering NSR, provided that the facility's "maximum hourly emissions achievable" after the changes were no greater than the same measure at any point during the past five years. By focusing on the hourly rate, rather than the previous measure (annual emissions), the new rule would effectively allow increases in annual emissions any time a modification led to an increase in the hours of operation of a facility. The agency's proposal stated that this change would establish a uniform national emissions test, in conformance with the Fourth Circuit's decision in the Duke Energy case, and it downplayed the significance of the change in light of "substantial emissions reductions from other CAA [Clean Air Act] requirements that are more efficient."

Since that time, both of these justifications have disappeared — the Fourth Circuit decision being overturned by the Supreme Court, and the "more efficient" reduction requirements (an allusion to CAIR) now being vacated by the D.C. Circuit. Internal EPA documents released by an environmental group have also indicated that the proposed rule was strongly opposed by the Air Enforcement Division, whose Director concluded that it would adversely affect the agency's NSR enforcement cases and is largely unenforceable as written.[77]

---

[75] State of New York v. EPA, No. 03-1380, 2006 Westlaw 662746 [D.C. Cir., March 17, 2006].

[76] 70 FR 61081, October 20, 2005 and 71 FR 54235, September 14, 2006. The September 2006 proposal would limit application of NSR by allowing plants to consider emissions only from the unit undergoing modification, rather than the entire plant, in determining whether NSR applies.

[77] Memorandum of Adam M. Kushner, Director, Air Enforcement Division, U.S. EPA, to William Harnett, Director, Information Transfer and Program Integration Division, Office of Air Quality Planning and Standards, August 25, 2005, p. 1.

Throughout the NSR debate, there appears to have been a conflict between the EPA's regulatory actions and its enforcement stance. While the agency stated in promulgating the equipment replacement rule that "we do not intend our actions today to create retroactive applicability for today's rule," continued pursuit of the enforcement actions filed during the Clinton Administration created a double standard for utilities, with one set of rules applicable to those utilities unlucky enough to have been cited for violations prior to promulgation of the new rule, and a different standard applicable afterward. Despite earlier agency denials that the rule would affect ongoing investigations, in early November 2003, the EPA's enforcement chief, J. P. Suarez, and another EPA official were reported to have indicated that the agency would drop enforcement actions against 47 facilities that had already received notices of violation, and would drop investigations of possible violations at an additional 70 power companies. Agency staff who were involved in the enforcement actions note that the prospect of NSR rollbacks has caused utilities already charged with violations to withdraw from settlement negotiations over the pending lawsuits, delaying emission reductions that could have been achieved.[78] (For additional information, see CRS Report RS21608, *Clean Air and New Source Review: Defining Routine Maintenance*, and CRS Report RL31757, *Clean Air: New Source Review Policies and Proposals*, by Larry Parker.)

At Congress's direction, the National Academy of Sciences began a review of the NSR program in May 2004. An interim report, released in January 2005, said the committee had not reached final conclusions, but it also said, "In general, NSR provides more stringent emission limits for new and modified major sources than EPA provides in other existing programs" and "It is ... unlikely that Clear Skies would result in emission limits at individual sources that are tighter than those achieved when NSR is triggered at the same sources."[79] The final report, issued July 21, 2006, found that

> [m]ore than 60% of all coal-fired electricity-generation capacity in the United States currently lacks the kinds of controls for SO_2 and NO_x emissions that have been required under NSR. Also, the older facilities are more likely than newer facilities to undergo maintenance, repair, and replacement of key components, so a substantial portion of emissions from the electricity-generating sector is potentially affected by the NSR rule changes.[80]

Nevertheless, the report reached ambivalent conclusions. On the one hand, the report stated, "It is reasonable to conclude that the implementation of the ERP [the proposed

---

[78] See, for example, "Departing EPA Official Issues Broadside at Administration Air, Enforcement Programs," *Daily Environment Report*, March 1, 2002, p. AA-1. Also, "Second Former EPA Enforcement Official Raps Bush's New Source Review Reforms," *Daily Environment Report*, October 22, 2002, p. A-9.

[79] National Research Council of the National Academies, *Interim Report of the Committee on Changes in New Source Review Programs for Stationary Sources of Air Pollutants* (Washington, DC: The National Academies Press, 2005), p. 27.

[80] National Research Council of the National Academies, *New Source Review for Stationary Sources of Air Pollutants* (Washington, DC: The National Academies Press, 2006), Prepublication Copy, p. 3.

Equipment Replacement Provision] could lead to SO_2 and NO_x emission increases in some locations and decreases in others."[81] On the other hand,

> the committee concluded overall that, because of a lack of data and the limitations of current models, it is not possible at this time to quantify with a reasonable degree of certainty the potential effects of the NSR rule changes on emissions, human health, energy efficiency, or on other relevant activities at facilities subject to the revised NSR program.[82]

Besides the NAS study, on April 21, 2003, the National Academy of Public Administration released a report commissioned by Congress that made sweeping recommendations to modify NSR. The study panel recommended that Congress end the "grandfathering" of major air emission sources by requiring all major sources that have not obtained an NSR permit since 1977 to install Best Available Control Technology or Lowest Achievable Emissions Rate control equipment. In the interim, the NAPA panel concluded, the EPA and the Department of Justice should continue to enforce NSR vigorously, especially for changes at existing facilities.[83]

---

[81] Ibid., p. 5.

[82] Ibid., p. 2.

[83] National Academy of Public Administration, *A Breath of Fresh Air: Reviving the New Source Review Program*, Summary Report, April 2003, p. 3.